Who Do You Say That I Am?

Charnette Kay

ISBN 979-8-89130-906-7 (paperback)
ISBN 979-8-89130-907-4 (digital)

Christian Faith Publishing
832 Park Avenue
Meadville, PA 16335
www.christianfaithpublishing.com

Printed in the United States of America

Special Thanks

Special thanks to my Lord and Savior, Jesus Christ. Thank You for who You are, in all Your glory. Thank you for every word You've spoken over my life and for every beautiful testimony. I treasure my relationship with You.

Thank you, Jay and Kenny, my handsome, powerful sons and personal miracles as a result of my conversations with God.

Thank you, Nyla, Nadia, Keon, and Jaliyah, my grandchildren, my sunshine. You make me want to be a better person.

Thank you, April R. Words cannot express my appreciation for the season God allowed us to share. He took us from a life-challenging season to a life-changing season before our very eyes. Favor and peace to you always. Thank you for being my sister in Christ.

Why This Type of Book?

I WROTE THIS BOOK BECAUSE I'VE seen what lies, jealousy, and control can do to people's relationships with their church family and their God. This book is a reminder that Christianity is based upon our relationship with God through His Son, Jesus Christ, and not based upon our relationship with Christ through His people.

I've witnessed and experienced so much disappointment, discouragement, and hurt within my Christian experience, but now that I'm made well, I can help bring people closer to God. I wanted to share my love relationship with Jesus as an example of how beautiful, mindful, and purposeful our fellowship with the Father can truly be. The Creator of the Universe loves us all, and He's concerned about everything that concerns us. No, we don't have all the answers. We never will. Instead, we get to exercise our faith every day. Sometimes we just have to settle in our hearts that God is sovereign, and in His infinite wisdom, He will have mercy upon whom He will have mercy and compassion upon whom He will have compassion, according to Romans 9:15.

These experiences and testimonies are based upon my love relationship with the Almighty God and are not meant to expose or show disrespect to anyone. This book is the result of journaling some of the worst seasons of my life, and through it all, I have come forth as pure gold. God is not a respecter of persons. What He'll do for one, He will do for another. As I read over these pages, I cried, remembering all the pain and disappointments, and then I laughed at the precious moments, being excited about God and amazed at His ability to just stop me in my tracks and capture my heart. Every day with Jesus is sweeter than the day before.

Be blessed and encouraged as you read. These words were written with you in mind.

Yahweh

I CAME ACROSS A BEAUTIFUL PICTURE of the names of God and had a blanket made. When I saw the first blanket, I loved it. It was so beautiful. I placed it on my bed and just thanked God and prayed over it. I felt the presence of the Lord, and I heard…

HOLY SPIRIT. Now pray that the names of God will manifest in your
   life and ministry.
ME. Oh, Lord!

I prayed and worshipped and cried. I gave one to my sister in Christ and told her what the Spirit of the Lord spoke to me. I have one, in my home, on the altar of the Lord, where it shall remain until Yahweh says otherwise.

Yahweh is the promised name of God. This name of God, which (by Jewish tradition) is too holy to voice, is actually spelled *YHWH* without vowels.

> So they got up early in the morning and went out into the Wilderness of Tekoa; and as they went out, Jehoshaphat stood and said, "Hear me, O Judah, and you inhabitants of Jerusalem! Believe and trust in the Lord your God and you will be established (secure). Believe and trust in His prophets and succeed." (2 Chronicles 20:20 AMP)

Writer

G OD WROTE THIS BOOK OVER the years. He asked me to start journaling, then when the time came to write, I had a lot of the pieces of the puzzle. After my birthday lunch, a friend presented me with a book to encourage new authors and a beautiful journal. Just what I needed to finish the project.

HER. I asked the Lord what to get for you and then He said that you could finish this book within thirty days.
ME. Hallelujah! It shall be done. (*After that, I got up and danced at the table.*)

God did it! I committed to waking up for the fourth watch prayer, between 3:00 a.m. and 6:00 a.m., and God multiplied my efforts. I never got discouraged. I had no more writer's block, fear, or intimidation about how my book would be received. It was evident that this was His project and not mine. That was all the assurance I needed to move forward.

ME. Lord, people are not going to believe some of these testimonies.
GOD. You write the book. I'll handle the people.

That means that if you're reading this book now, God is with you now. He's handling you and dealing with you right where you are. Maybe you don't believe me. Maybe you don't believe in God. Maybe I'm experiencing the life you forfeited through fear, sin, doubt, and unbelief. Maybe this is confirmation for you that you're not crazy after all, and God really does speak to you, that He cares about even the little things in your life. Maybe this is all peanuts for you and you were born in the arms of Jesus. Either way, give yourself a big hug from me. You are not forgotten. You are so special to God, and you are loved. He encouraged me to write this book, but He had you on His mind.

> Then the LORD answered me and said: "Write the vision And make *it* plain on tablets, That he may run who reads it." (Habakkuk 2:2 NKJV)

Visionary

My writing flourished with a long-distance relationship many years ago. It was expensive to talk on the phone then and time-consuming to wait for letters to come in the mail. I would write him letters that I never planned to send. Letters turned into poetry, and then God got involved.

He focused my gaze upon Him, and I wrote day and night about the presence and power of God in my life. I was fulfilled and transformed as I read scripture(s) and wrote articles, letters, and testimonies to the glory of God. Writing is therapeutic for me. For about ten years, whenever you would see me, I had a pen in my hair or in my hand. I would even stand up to the microphone to sing or speak with an ink pen in my right hand. It became such a beautiful habit for me, and the ideas, words, and love would easily flow from my heart to my fingers. I've always been an author; it's just now time to get published.

> I am convinced *and* confident of this very thing, that He who has begun a good work in you will [continue to] perfect *and* complete it until the day of Christ Jesus [the time of His return]. (Philippians 1:6 AMP)

Truth

My dad was sick, and church members, family, and friends came to our home to pray for him and give well wishes. There was a lot of confusion, declarations, and decrees going forth. Will he live, or will he die? I went into my room and prepared myself for the answer.

Me. Lord, what's going on here? Is my dad going to live?
God. Make his last days pleasurable.
Me. Okay. Thank You.

When everyone left, I told my family what the Lord said, so at least we could all be on the same page. Later, I prepared my dad's feet for the podiatrist. I found a basin, sat on the floor, and washed and dried my dad's feet. When I was done, he looked down at me with love in his eyes.

Dad. Nobody's ever done anything like that for me before. Thank you.
Me. You're welcome.

I helped him get back in bed and gathered my supplies. I walked away with tears in my eyes.

Me. That was it, Lord. I did it. That was what I could do to help make his last days pleasurable.

My dad passed away within three weeks, but God prepared and settled my heart. Thank You, Lord, for truth!

> Jesus said to him, "I am the [only] Way [to God] and the [real] Truth and the [real] Life; no one comes to the Father but through Me." (John 14:6 AMP)

Travel Agent

I HAD A DREAM I WAS in the local mall, pointing at a brown leather bag. Looking closer in the dream, I saw that the briefcase had a map of the world on it. I had pointed out some places I had been. The dream was so real that I went to the handbag kiosk in the local mall, where I was standing in my dream. I described the briefcase to the saleslady. It wasn't on display, so I told her about my dream. She had the bag, locked in the bottom cabinet, and got it for me.

ME. Thank you so much. This is it.

I was determined to buy it, no matter the cost. I brought it home and prayed over God's travel plans for me. Weeks later, someone broke into my car and stole my new briefcase. I went back to the same kiosk in the local mall to see if they had another briefcase. Once again, the bag was not on display, yet there was a second bag locked in the bottom cabinet. I bought that one too.

Everything God has for us is for us. If we don't give up our promises through fear, sin, doubt, or unbelief, surely no one can take them away from us. Nothing and no one has the power nor the authority to take anything that God has for us. I receive all God's travel plans for me as already done! I already saw it, and it is so, in Jesus's name.

> And He said, "Hear now My words: If there
> is a prophet among you, I the LORD will make
> Myself known to him in a vision And I will speak
> to him in a dream." (Numbers 12:6 AMP)

The Same God

My sons are twenty years apart, and one day my infant had a fever that just would not break. I left a message for the nurse to call me back immediately. It was in the middle of the night, and I was getting impatient, frustrated, and starting to panic.

God. Am I not the same God?

Me. The same God?

God. Yes, am I not the same God? Twenty years ago, you stayed up all night with Me, praying for the baby, lifting him up to Me, asking Me to break the fever and heal him. But now that you have a husband and health insurance, instead of giving him to Me, you're upset because you're not getting a phone call back from a nurse who cannot heal him.

Ouch!

Me. Yes, Lord, please forgive me. You are the same God. Thank You for being with us. Break this fever once again and heal my son, in Jesus's name, amen.

God did the miraculous for both of us that night. He came all the way through for my son and helped me to cultivate my love relationship with Him and taught me to perfect my worship.

> Jesus Christ is [eternally changeless, always]
> the same yesterday and today and forever.
> (Hebrews 13:8 AMP)

The Most High

SOMEONE HAD THE BRIGHT IDEA of coming up with a business name similar to mine, in the same county, with the purpose of misleading my customers and stealing business. Some of my previous customers knew it was not me upon arrival. Some canceled their appointments, and some let it be, but I was more concerned about what God had to say.

ME. Lord, I know they tried to benefit from my name and steal business from me. I can contact my clients and prove it, but what do You want me to do?
GOD. As long as you do what I tell you to do, you will never have any competition.
ME. Okay, Lord. Thank You. Well, I will never have any competition.

Over the next few months, as people continued to talk about the situation, I took pleasure in repeating what my Father said to me. It ended up being a blessing for them so that they too would know that as long as they are obedient to the Word of the Lord, they will have no competition as well.

Four years later, a young lady walked into the office and confirmed what I was thinking all along. I handed her one of my business cards.

HER. It's you?
ME. Yes, I'm Charnette, but what do you mean?
HER. I used to work for a certain business, and I can confirm that they purposely used a name close enough to yours and made contracts with the same company, for the purpose of stealing

your business. They saw your reviews and set out to offer your clients discounts as they came in.

Me. Thank you for that. You confirmed what I already knew. I prayed about it, and my Father told me as long as I do what He tells me to do, I will never have any competition. Therefore, they don't have the ability to take anything from me, and they never will. I have no competition, and I never will.

She looked at me like I was being arrogant. I looked at her like… I know who my Father is, and I know He has the last word on my business. Any questions?

May you have no competition ever in the things God has called you to do.

> I will cry to God Most High,
> Who accomplishes *all things* on my behalf [for
> He completes my purpose in His plan].
> He will send from heaven and save me;
> He calls to account him who tramples me down.
> Selah.
> God will send out His lovingkindness and His
> truth.
> My life is among lions;
> I must lie among those who breathe out fire—
> The sons of men whose teeth are spears and arrows,
> And their tongue a sharp sword.
> Be exalted above the heavens, O God;
> Let Your glory *and* majesty be over all the earth.
> They set a net for my steps;
> My very life was bowed down.
> They dug a pit before me;
> Into the midst of it they themselves have fallen.
> Selah.
> (Psalm 57:2–6)

The King of Glory

I WAS IN A VERY HEATED conversation with one of my natural enemies, who was trying to stand in the way of the perfect will of God in my life. I didn't know how much of an attack I was under until about seven years later. However, I was well-equipped with my spiritual arsenal: prayer, praise, and my heavenly language.

It got so intense that I had to pull over, park, and turn my car off to step out and finish my conversation. A woman came out of her home, looked around, and then watched me from her porch. I saw her, yet I could not give her my attention because I was focused on my conversation. When I was done, she called out to me, and our conversation went something like this.

HER. Are you okay? Is everything okay?
ME. Oh, yes, ma'am. It's alright now!
HER. God told me to get up and come outside to see the glory of the Lord. Look at it out here. Look how bright and beautiful it is out here.
ME. Well, hallelujah!

I was so engaged in warfare that I hadn't noticed. We looked up and down the street. The whole atmosphere had changed. The cars, the homes, the trees had all been covered in the glory. Everything was illuminated with the brilliance of God.

We praised the Lord together, and I finally drove away. My passenger fell asleep for about an hour. They couldn't function under that much power. Hallelujah!

Your spiritual arsenal is greater than screaming out for help. God will surely send someone to see about you.

> The weapons of our warfare are not physical [weapons of flesh and blood]. Our weapons are divinely powerful for the destruction of fortresses. (2 Corinthians 10:4 AMP)

The God Who Sees

I WOULD GO TO ONE MALL every month, over the course of a year, to get my nails done. Each time I got my nails done, I would stop by the jewelry store to visit this beautiful two-carat diamond engagement ring. I had never seen a ring like this before. It was an original, and I would have to go to the jeweler who made it to create a matching wedding band. I just know what I like, and this was it.

When I saw the ring, I was overwhelmed with joy and felt like I just had to have it. I knew it was for me. I would pose with this ring on my finger and walk around the store. It got to the point where the salespeople knew who I was, and they would take the ring out even as they saw me approaching the store. I would make declarations over the ring like…

ME. Oh, when my husband comes, he's going to buy me this engagement ring. When my husband comes, he's going to know right away that this is my ring. When my husband comes, he's going to pick out this ring at first glance.

I started dating in May. The gentleman asked me to marry him in July. I said yes, and in August, I took him to the ring store. I asked the sales lady to line up all the rings, and out of about ninety rings, he picked out "my ring" on the first guess. I was so happy and surprised.

ME. How did you know?
HIM. I already saw it on your finger.

I knew I was getting married, and this was my ring. When we decided to officially be engaged, we could not afford the ring, but we trusted God. He found a ring at the same store that he really liked, and we just prayed about it.

I went back again after getting my nails done to check on the ring, and someone had placed it on layaway. I gave the saleslady my name and phone number and asked her to please call me when they give this ring back because this ring is truly mine. She looked at me like I was crazy, but she put my name in the lay-a-way bag with the ring. About three weeks later, she gave me a call.

SALESLADY. You were absolutely right. They no longer want this ring. I guess it is yours.
ME. Hallelujah! See you tomorrow.

We were there within twenty-four hours to put a deposit on the rings. God had given us a strategy for the finances and made a way to pay for the rings in full.

> Then she called the name of the LORD who spoke to her, "You are God Who Sees"; for she said, "Have I not even here [in the wilderness] remained alive after seeing Him [who sees me with understanding and compassion]?" (Genesis 16:13 AMP)

The Christ

WE ARE ONE WITH THE Father because of Christ. By Jesus's stripes, we were healed. Who will be healed through His stripes? I will be healed through His stripes! I have a story to tell. Don't you? Don't we all? Why wait? That's the treasure that's in this earthen vessel. Christ, God's anointed, full of grace and truth, has all the power to endure (through us) the hurt, pain, disappointment, rejection, and everything and anything else we're still here to endure. 1 Corinthians 10:13 says:

> No temptation [regardless of its source] has overtaken *or* enticed you that is not common to human experience [nor is any temptation unusual or beyond human resistance]; but God is faithful [to His word—He is compassionate and trustworthy], and He will not let you be tempted beyond your ability [to resist], but along with the temptation He [has in the past and is now and] will [always] provide the way out as well, so that you will be able to endure it [without yielding, and will overcome temptation with joy].

It doesn't feel good when we're going through it, but God always gives us victory, and we overcome temptation (through Him) with joy. Everything we've been through was necessary. God doesn't tell us the whole story. We just have to trust Him, exercise our faith, and believe He's going to bring us all the way through, in His own time. There's nothing that I would change about the hardships, disappointments, struggles, or difficulties in my life because it's all working together for my good. It was confusing and painful there for a season or two, but today I appreciate it all. Maybe if I share my story and help someone, they will share their story and help more people, and we could all be living our best life in Christ.

We all have the examples, the experiences, and the proof that when you trust in God, you can never fail. You'll never even really fall. God will always prevail. No matter what. Christ's blood is sufficient for every sin and transgression. He already made provision for our shortcomings, sins, and even the weights that we like to hold on to for some reason. Christ paid it all in full before we even had an opportunity to mess things up.

> But He was wounded for our transgressions,
> He was crushed for our wickedness [our sin,
> our injustice, our wrongdoing]; The punishment
> [required] for our well-being fell on Him, And by
> His stripes (wounds) we are healed. (Isaiah 53:5
> AMP)

Look at how the punishment that was required for us fell on Him so that we could be well and whole, free in our mind, body, and soul. And by His stripes or wounds, we are even now healed. Regardless of what it looks like. Regardless of what it feels like. Allow the Word of God to bypass your flesh so you can stand in victory every day, in every way, in Jesus's name.

Show some gratitude, celebrate, rejoice, and be thankful for your victory in Christ. After all, it's not about us; we stand in awe of Christ's sufficiency!

> In every situation [no matter what the cir-
> cumstances] be thankful *and* continually give
> thanks *to God*; for this is the will of God for you
> in Christ Jesus. (1 Thessalonians 5:18 AMP)

Sweet Surprise

HOLY SPIRIT SAYS IT'S TIME to fast. For me, that generally means no food for forty days. Nobody signs up for this class. But for me, it's been a requirement and has been for the past ten years. Well, I'm older now. I'm not looking forward to the negative changes that happen in my body, and besides, I just bought Popeyes chicken. I didn't know that was going to be my last meal until day 41.

This time, Jesus became and still is my *sweet surprise*. This has been the best consecration experience ever. I was able to get plenty of rest. I was able to worship, read, and pray uninterrupted. My son became more responsible with helping around the house and took the initiative to add more chores for himself during the week. I took more contract work, and God blessed me with one-hour commutes (to increase our private time). I did not suffer, I wasn't hungry, I didn't lose my taste buds or sense of smell, there was no dehydration or cramping, and now I know Him in the most miraculous way.

I received blessing after blessing during this time of fasting and prayer, but no gift nor surprise will ever take the place of Jesus the Christ, the Son of the Living God.

For with God nothing [is or ever] shall be impossible. (Luke 1:37 AMP)

Supplier

I PICKED UP DINNER FROM ONE of my favorite restaurants. I had forgotten I had a gift certificate waiting for me for several weeks. I asked about it when I got there. The gentleman didn't know what I was talking about, so he took my name and number.

HIM. I'll find out what's going on and call you tomorrow.
ME. Okay, thank you.

He called the next day. I missed his call, but when I called back, I went ahead and ordered food.

A young lady took my order and told me my gift certificate was there in a sealed envelope. When I got there, she gave me my food and the envelope and told me to have a nice day. I tried to pay. I started opening the envelope to use the gift certificate, but she would not allow me to pay with my gift certificate. This woman actually walked away from me backward, while telling me to have a nice day.

HER. Thank you so much and have a nice day.
ME. But I can…
HER. Thank you, ma'am. Have a nice day.

I stood there looking lost and finally said thank you and wished her a nice day. She acted like she was not allowed to take my money. Well, thank You, Daddy. The gift certificate was for forgetting a side order on my last carry-out meal. When I opened the envelope, it was enough for two full meals. Thank You, Lord!

> Give, and it will be given to you. They will pour into your lap a good measure—pressed down, shaken together, and running over [with no space left for more]. For with the standard of measurement you use [when you do good to others], it will be measured to you in return. (Luke 6:38 AMP)

Sovereign

I RELUCTANTLY TOOK ON THE TASK of teaching children's church. I felt so unworthy and unqualified, but there was a need, and someone had to do it.

GOD. There is a "due" season and a "what I will do for you" season. ME. Okay, Lord, I'll do it.

God gave me wisdom and strategy. Every child played a part in the Bible teachings so that they all were able to comprehend. The youngest had to explain what was read and acted out to show that they really understood. They were all engaged and excited to participate.

At the end of the semester, every child from five to twelve years old had received salvation and was baptized. The pastor continued to ask the youngest student about Christ, to make sure she understood the plan of salvation and not just agreeing with everyone else. Her response went a little something like this...

PASTOR. (*in her voice*) Pastor, if you ask me that one more time... I told you I love God and Jesus is in my heart.

Imagine a forty-five-year-old man speaking with a lisp, in a five-year-old girl's voice. Hilarious, right? She was saved and baptized with the rest of the children. To God be the glory for the great things He has done.

> Preach the word [as an official messenger];
> be ready when the time is right and even when

it is not [keep your sense of urgency, whether the opportunity seems favorable or unfavorable, whether convenient or inconvenient, whether welcome or unwelcome]; correct [those who err in doctrine or behavior], warn [those who sin], exhort and encourage [those who are growing toward spiritual maturity], with inexhaustible patience and [faithful] teaching. (2 Timothy 4:2 AMP)

Savior

IN CELEBRATION OF MY WOMEN'S ministry, I bought a sheet cake, and the ladies and I planned a luncheon at a local restaurant. Many who were invited did not attend, so we decided to be a blessing to the customers. We offered them cake and witnessed the Good News of Jesus Christ.

I met someone who also celebrated the start of her women's ministry at the same restaurant many years prior. We congratulated one another, and she shared her testimony. A pastor friend ministered to Christ and prayed the prayer of salvation with one of the employees. Glory to God!

The day didn't go as we planned it, but God had a much greater plan.

> Many plans are in a man's mind, but it is the LORD's purpose for him that will stand (be carried out). (Proverbs 19:21 AMP)

Salvation

Jesus is Lord of all, the Way, the Truth, and the Life (Romans 10:12, John 14:6).

He will not give us the whole story so that we may be sure to have confidence, faith, and trust in Him. He has made all things beautiful in His own time, all things (Ecclesiastes 3:11). So you can just speak what it is you want to see for your life. We walk by faith and not by sight (2 Corinthians 5:7.) We are free in Christ to speak those things that are not as though they are (Romans 4:17).

I pray the perfect will of God for your life. The hurdles aren't easy; training never is, but there can be joy on the other side, the other side of yourself, your feelings, your attitude, and your motives concerning the things ahead. In the midst of God's great work, He has a way of changing us so we can change our circumstances. I pray you give permission for Jesus to be Lord in your life. He will make you fearless and unstoppable.

He wants everything to work for your good (Romans 8:28). May the Lord perfect those things concerning you (Psalm 138:8). May He cause you to have no limitations and no barriers in your future. May He do new things for you and make ways for you where there seems to be no way (Isaiah 43:19). He's the God of more than enough, the God of all flesh (Jeremiah 32:27), and the exceeding, abundant God (Ephesians 3:20–21). Let Him love you, shape, make, and mold you. Jesus knows your ending from your beginning, and He knows your whole story. Won't you rather wake up in the loving arms of Jesus Christ, your Savior, and be refreshed, be restored, be comforted, be delivered? May you be filled with power, energy, and abundant life. You have the ability and capacity already inside of you to do all things through Christ (Philippians 4:13). He does all things well, and He makes all things new (2 Corinthians 5:17).

In whatever state you find yourself in, you can learn to be content and excel (Philippians 4:11–13). Move with the purpose, authority, and the anointing of Christ. Be crucified in your flesh and live your glorified life today. How? By the faith of the Son of God who loves you and gave His life for you (Galatians 2:20). He whom the Son has set free is free indeed (John 8:36). Be free in Jesus's name.

It is that easy. In this life, you will have trouble (John 16:32), but it's definitely worth it. Jesus has all power, and that power is at work within you, Christian soldier (Matthew 28:18–20). You can take as long as you like by doing things your own way. But why put off 'til tomorrow what you can do today?

If you have not received Jesus Christ as your personal Lord and Savior, you can pray this simple but powerful prayer:

Heavenly Father, thank You for who You are in all Your glory. I come in the name of Jesus in need of forgiveness, in need of a Savior. I repent of my sins and transgressions. Please forgive me and have me as Your own. I believe in Jesus's virgin birth, death, and resurrection. Jesus, I believe You are the Son of God, and I receive You now into my heart and make You my Lord and Savior. Cleanse me in Your blood and make me a new creation in You. Help me to live my life by faith in You. Give me the grace to go and sin no more and thank You for it all, in the mighty name of Jesus, amen.

I pray that God will lead you and guide you into all truth and fill you daily with His Holy Spirit. Go forth in faith and full assurance that in Him you live, move, and have your being.

> For it is by grace [God's remarkable compassion and favor drawing you to Christ] that you have been saved [actually delivered from judgment and given eternal life] through faith. And this [salvation] is not of yourselves [not through your own effort], but it is the [undeserved, gracious] gift of God; not as a result of [your] works [nor your attempts to keep the Law], so that no

one will [be able to] boast or take credit in any way [for his salvation]. (Ephesians 2:8–9 AMP)

If you are living habitually outside of the will of God, and you'd like to rededicate your life to Jesus Christ, you can pray this simple but powerful prayer:

> Heavenly Father, thank You for who You are in all Your glory. I come in the name of Jesus in need of forgiveness. I repent of my sins and transgressions. Please forgive me, and receive me back as Your own. Cleanse me in Your blood, and make me a new creation in You. Help me to live my life by faith in You. Give me the Grace to go and sin no more and thank You for it all, in the mighty name of Jesus, amen.

I pray that God will lead you and guide you into all truth and fill you daily with His Holy Spirit. Go forward in faith and full assurance that what God has started within you, He is able to complete.

> Call to Me and I will answer you, and tell you [and even show you] great and mighty things, [things which have been confined and hidden], which you do not know and understand and cannot distinguish. (Jeremiah 33:3 AMP)

Realtor

I WAS BROWSING THE INTERNET, LOOKING at homes.

GOD. That's your house.
ME. This is my house?
GOD. Yes.
ME. Can I see it?
GOD. Yes.

I printed out the picture of the house with all the information, took it home, and set it on my altar. Everywhere I live, I build an altar to the Lord with the Bible opened to a particular scripture, verse, or promise. I set my prayers and expectations all around it and thank God in advance for all that He's done, all that He's doing, and all that He's going to do.

I anointed my apartment keys for divine exchange, thanked God in advance for my new home, and started packing in faith. I was led to all the right people at the right times. I had favor everywhere I went. I wasn't familiar with the home-buying process, but my experience was nothing like what I had heard. Settlement was faster and easier than anyone said it would be. All parties were present, and we were done within two hours. I put no money down and, to my surprise, I was given a check. Everything fell right into place. The gas and electric were even in my name before I left the office.

> And not a creature exists that is concealed
> from His sight, but all things are open and exposed,
> and revealed to the eyes of Him with whom we
> have to give account. (Hebrews 4:13 AMP)

Psalmist

I WAS DRYING MY HAIR UNDER a hooded dryer and heard a beautiful song. I lifted up the hood and listened to see if the song was on the radio, playing in the background. The radio was playing a different song, so I put the hood back down and proceeded to let my hair dry. I heard again this beautiful melody.

ME. Lord, what is that?
GOD. Grab your word. Turn to this scripture.

As I listened to the tune in my own head, I started getting the words to match, and I heard this beautiful voice. The voice I hear is so sweet and pure that I have yet to realize that it's me singing. It was the voice of my youth before I started singing hard gospel music.

ME. What? This is my song, Lord?
GOD. Turn to this scripture.

I grabbed a pen and paper and started writing what I heard.

GOD. Turn here.
ME. Wow! This is beautiful, Lord. Thank You.

I was getting married in a few months, and my mother wanted me to walk down the aisle to the traditional "Bridal Chorus" song; however, the organist didn't show. I had a few seconds to decide how I was going to walk down the aisle. I asked for a microphone and sang the song of the Lord.

God had given me the lyrics and melody so I could sing to Him His own song as I walked down the aisle.

Hallelujah!

> The LORD your God is with you, the Mighty Warrior who saves. He will take great delight in you; in his love he will no longer rebuke you, but will rejoice over you with singing. (Zephaniah 3:17 NIV)

Present

THE TIME HAD COME FOR me to leave my apartment. I had been there for about two and a half years, and the area was getting really bad.

ME. Lord, whatever door You open for us, I'm gonna take it.

Not many days later, a woman came in for a massage, and we quickly got acquainted. She ended up having a bad experience in the same area where I lived and offered to stay in her basement apartment. She described the five-acre property, and the basement had two bedrooms and a full bathroom. Not many days later, I went to her home to check it out.

ME. Lord, this is really fast, but is this the door that You have for us?
    Is this where You want us to be?
GOD. I will be with you wherever you go.
ME. Okay, let's go. Thank You.

It was a fast move because it was no longer safe to live in my area. My son was in one school on Friday and in a new school on Monday morning. God was and still is with us.

> God is our refuge and strength [mighty and
> impenetrable], A very present and well-proved
> help in trouble. (Psalm 46:1b AMP)

Prayer-Answering God

I WENT TO A RESTAURANT WITH a friend and asked the Lord for His favor. The parking lot was full, and we just didn't want to wait a long time. The hostess said it would be at least twenty minutes. I got some earrings and a Chick-O-Stick and left for another restaurant.

I AM. Didn't you ask Me to favor you? They said twenty minutes, but I didn't.
ME. I'm so sorry, Lord. Do You want us to go back?
I AM. You can do what you want to do, but you left without giving Me an opportunity. Some things don't apply to you. Somebody else may have to wait twenty minutes, but not you.
ME. Wow! Thank You, Lord. Continue to help me and challenge me in this. I need You, Lord. Help me to walk in Your favor.

> For the Lord God is a sun and shield; The Lord bestows grace and favor and honor; No good thing will He withhold from those who walk uprightly. (Psalms 84:11–12 AMP)

Powerful

The following year, after fasting for forty days with no food, I felt like the Lord was calling me to do it again. It started on December 26 and ended on February 4. This year, in particular, God was having His way with me. I had to follow Him through some places I didn't want to go. I was even surprised He was there. I made the best of Christmas dinner. I would smile and greet our guests, be cordial and warm while burying my true feelings and biting my lip all the way.

A friend made the best ham I had ever had. It was unbelievably good. That was the best part of my Christmas dinner experience; my attitude had greatly improved. Ham has a way of doing that. The next day, I had ham and eggs for breakfast, a ham sandwich for lunch, and ham with the other leftovers for dinner. The fast was to start at 6:00 p.m. I was so happy and satisfied.

Me. Lord, this ham is so good. I don't think I can do the fast this year.
God. You didn't do it last year.
Me. Hallelujah! Do it again, Lord!

> I can do all things [which He has called me to do] through Him who strengthens and empowers me [to fulfill His purpose—I am self-sufficient in Christ's sufficiency; I am ready for anything and equal to anything through Him who infuses me with inner strength and confident peace.] (Philippians 4:13 AMP)

Those words carried me all the way through to day 41. He had done it again, through me. Glory to God!

Power

I was afraid of heights, yet I refused to be overcome with fear. I bought a Groupon for two, to fly over our city for a romantic, backseat tour. I thought it was a good idea to just relax, take pictures, and let someone else take the wheel.

My significant other was not interested in getting into such a small plane, so a coworker came with me. I ended up sitting up front with the pilot, and he let me fly the plane. It was weird, and I was awkward, but at least there was nothing to hit. I kept looking over the dashboard as if someone was going to pull out in front of me.

The pilot was so relaxed and friendly. I had most of the same buttons on my side as he had on his, and he taught me some things that I'd soon forget. We flew for about two hours, and the spirit of fear that once overcame me was gone, and I had the victory. I was no longer afraid of heights.

We landed the plane, and I felt like there was nothing I could not do. I'd like to get my pilot's license someday.

> For God did not give us a spirit of timidity or cowardice or fear, but [He has given us a spirit] of power and of love and of sound judgment and personal discipline [abilities that result in a calm, well-balanced mind and self-control]. (2 Timothy 1:7 AMP)

Peace

Someone charged $4,500 worth of fraudulent charges on my debit card. I had to answer all the questions concerning my claim, and I was told it might take thirty to forty days to receive my reimbursement, after investigation. God led me to all the proof I needed to show that I had nothing to do with it. The bank had closed temporarily within two days of the incident, and apparently, other people had been affected as well. I faxed all the paperwork I collected concerning my claim and prayed.

Me. No delay, no delay, no delay on my full reimbursement in Jesus' name. (*for at least five days*)

I had so much peace because I knew the Lord was with me. I ended up receiving all of my reimbursements within two weeks. Hallelujah!

May you receive back (in not many days) everything that the enemy has stolen or hidden from you, even seven times more, in Jesus's name, amen.

> Do not be anxious or worried about anything, but in everything [every circumstance and situation] by prayer and petition with thanksgiving, continue to make your [specific] requests known to God. And the peace of God [that peace which reassures the heart, that peace] which transcends all understanding, [that peace which] stands guard over your hearts and your minds in Christ Jesus [is yours]. (Philippians 4:6–7 AMP)

Owner

I WAS AT WORK ONE DAY, having a spiritual conversation with someone when a coworker walked in with the purpose of mocking our conversation. He knew I was a believer in Christ and tried to make light of my relationship with God. That day, there was thundering, lightning, and heavy rain outside.

COWORKER. You know Him. You should tell Him to do something about all that rain outside.

I just looked at him. I had a heavy heart because of the nerve of this man, but I couldn't think of anything clever to say. I went into my workroom and shut the door.

ME. Oh, Father, it would be so good if You would cause all the thunder, rain, and lightning to go away. Father, please make the sun shine like it has never shone before. Oh, God, it would be so good if You would just create a miracle in the face of this man who is trying to make a mockery of my relationship with Christ. It would be so good if You would just make the sun shine so bright that it's undeniable. Thank You, Lord. This is my prayer, in Jesus's name, amen.

After about an hour, the Lord prompted me to look outside. He did it for me! The sun was ridiculously bright. Everybody was shocked because of how quickly the whole atmosphere changed. I was with a client and unable to see the actual transition from storm to calm, but I was in *awe*!

ME. Hey, did you look outside?
COWORKER. (*He ran to the front door and ran back to me.*) What? Did
    you see that sun?
ME. Yeah. I know the Owner.

> The earth is the LORD's, and the fullness of
> it, The world, and those who dwell in it. (Psalm
> 24:1 AMP)

I walked away like it was nothing, but I wanted to scream. I went back to my workroom and tried my best to hold it all in. I was clapping, walking in circles, and thanking God. I loved it. The look on his face was priceless. He never said another negative word to me again. Actually, I don't think he ever spoke to me again. Oh well, God is still speaking to me, and that's what really matters.

My Treasure

I WENT TO THE GROCERY STORE to get my favorite drink. I grabbed bottles and the fifth one looked like it had been stepped on by a three-hundred-pound man in a pair of steel-toed boots, by mistake, in the dark. So I put the fifth one back.

GOD. The contents are still good.
ME. But it's messed up on the outside.
GOD. But the contents are still good.
ME. I don't know, Lord. (*Inspecting the bottle*) What is this…mud?
GOD. The contents are still good. Isn't that how people looked at you? Pushed you aside. Disregarded you?
ME. Well…
GOD. They didn't know that the contents are still good.
ME. Hallelujah! (*Holding back my tears*)

I grabbed that fifth bottle, paid for my drink, and praised God all the way to my car. I remembered all the rejection, confusion, misunderstanding, and loneliness that I had gone through. I remembered all the people, places, and things. I washed that bottle off, praised God for it, and put it in my refrigerator. God saved that ugly bottle just for me. After all, I was the ugly bottle that Jesus saved, just for Him. Hallelujah!

I don't have a problem anymore with bent cans and damaged labels nor do I have a problem with broken thought patterns and damaged people. I'm always reminded of the contents on the inside.

But we have this precious treasure [the good
news about salvation] in [unworthy] earthen ves-

sels [of human frailty], so that the grandeur and surpassing greatness of the power will be [shown to be] from God [His sufficiency] and not from ourselves. (2 Corinthians 4:7 AMP)

My Rest

Tʜɪs ɪs ᴀ sᴇᴀsᴏɴ ᴏꜰ rest for me, and I've been getting it in. I'm so proud of myself because now I look forward to winding down for the evening. When I get in, I rarely leave out again. I had gone to the water (my happy place) to just love on the Lord and appreciate His work. It started to drizzle after about an hour. I decided to run to the store before I went in for the morning. As soon as I put my car in park, it started to pour down rain.

Mᴇ. Lord, what is this?
Lᴏʀᴅ. I told you to rest!
Mᴇ. Wow! Okay.

It's not so much about what I was doing; it was more about what I wasn't doing. Being wise with my time was not the problem. God just needs to know that I am willing to follow His directions, without being distracted. I appreciate my correction. I just felt bad for the people that got rained on. It was so sudden, and they were not prepared for it.

Sometimes what we do really does affect other people, like in the book of Jonah.

> Jonah said to them, "Pick me up and throw me into the sea. Then the sea will become calm for you, for I know that it is because of me that this great storm has come upon you." (Jonah 1:12 AMP)

My Leader

I WAS HAVING A REALLY TOUGH time in my marriage. I was faced with things that only God could help with, and He would periodically check on me.

GOD. You okay?
ME. Yes, Father. I'm good. I know You don't like divorce. I'm going to hang in there. I'm fine. Just help me through.

Here comes something else in not many days. I'm on the floor, weeping again, crying, hurting, and disappointed.

GOD. You alright?
ME. Yes, sir. I'm okay. I know You don't like divorce. I'm fine. I'll get it together. I'll pray. I'll hang in there. I don't want to disappoint You.

Here comes something else, in not many days.

GOD: You okay?
ME. No, sir. I'm ready. I'm done.
GOD. Okay, follow me.

Not many days later, my husband received a four-page text, and he was in the shower.

GOD: You need to see that.
ME. No thanks. I'm good.

God. You need to see that.

Me. Okay.

By then I was wrapped up in Jesus and had peace, and it didn't really matter what was going to become of my marriage. As I read the text, I realized it was grounds for divorce.

Me. Hallelujah!

I'm still following God with no regrets. He was done with our marriage long before I was. I have my *takeaway* from the marriage, our son.

> Then Jesus said to His disciples, "If anyone wishes to follow Me [as My disciple], he must deny himself [set aside selfish interests], and take up his cross [expressing a willingness to endure whatever may come] and follow Me [believing in Me, conforming to My example in living and, if need be, suffering or perhaps dying because of faith in Me]." (Matthew 16:24 AMP)

My Future

God sent me to massage therapy school. I was so excited. I had been wanting to go for years but couldn't fit it into my schedule and budget. Finally, I had toured the school and came to the point of filling out the application and paying the application fee. My cell phone rang.

Me. Excuse me, please. This is my husband. Hello?
Him. Pay the lady.
Me. Excuse me?
Him. Pay the lady.
Me. Okay. Anything else?
Him. No.

I contained myself as best I could and paid the lady. I was finally enrolled. Hallelujah!

> "For I know the plans and thoughts that I have for you," says the Lord, "plans for peace and well-being and not for disaster, to give you a future and a hope." (Jeremiah 29:11 AMP)

My Delight

I WAS ALL SET TO DANCE at the evening service. It was my special offering to the Lord on Mother's Day. I was nervous but confident that God would get the glory! After all, He spoke a promise over my dance, and since then, several prophecies over my feet. I wore a beautiful, white pair of five-inch heels. I stepped down and twisted my right ankle on a crack in the pavement. Looking back, I realized I could have fallen or really injured myself. I was also holding my three-year-old's hand, but we were both just fine.

ME. Devil, I rebuke you in the name of Jesus. I will dance today, and God will get the glory! No sprain, no pain, no swelling, in Jesus's name. I will dance today!

I praised God right up to the start of the next service, and when I realized the devil was possibly trying to shut down the promise of God, I really got bold. By the enemy trying to attack me, he was actually validating the promise of God attached to my dance.

ME. I declare victory over my ankles, my feet, and the dance, in Jesus's name.

When the time came, I introduced my new dance ministry and shared the testimony of how God sent a stranger to confirm how serious He was about my dancing. It was a prophetic expression of victory, and God kept His promise. He sent a mighty deliverance and changed the atmosphere and the whole order of service. To God be the glory for the great things He has done!

May you have special grace to persevere because of your obedience to the Word of God, In Jesus's name, amen.

> The steps of a [good and righteous] man are
> directed *and* established by the Lord, And He
> delights in his way [and blesses his path]. (Psalm
> 37:23 AMP)

My Conscience

I WENT TO THE BANK AND made a $600 deposit. I got there just in time before they closed. The teller gave me back a fat envelope with all my $20s in it as well as my deposit receipt for $600.

ME. Is she serious, Lord?

She turned off the outside lights and closed the blinds on the window. I honked the horn several times. She finally acknowledged me as if I was bothering her.

ME. You gave me all my money back.
HER. Excuse me?
ME. I gave you the $600, and you gave it all back to me. I have my deposit receipt, that's correct, but please take this money back.
HER. Oh no! I'm so sorry. Thank you very much.
ME. You are more than welcome. Have a nice day!

I pulled off the parking lot feeling like heaven was smiling upon me. I had no intentions of keeping the money. I didn't know whether I was being tested by the Father or tempted by the devil. But I'm not moved by money, so I quickly passed the test.

No temptation [regardless of its source] has overtaken or enticed you that is not common to human experience [nor is any temptation unusual or beyond human resistance]; but God is faithful [to His word—He is compassionate and trustworthy], and He will not let you be tempted beyond your ability [to resist], but along with the temptation He [has in the past and is now and] will [always] provide the way out as well, so that you will be able to endure it [without yielding, and will overcome temptation with joy]." (1 Corinthians 10:13 AMP)

Miraculous

I RECEIVED A CALL TO PRAY for someone who had sustained a brain injury and was in a coma. He fell from the roof of a hospital while working. The fact that he was so close to help really saved his life.

I was driving when I received the call, but when I felt a pull physically, I pulled over so I could focus and pray. I saw a vision of the patient, spoke to his soul man, and called him by name. I continued until I saw some response from him (in the spirit); first, his feet moved and then his hands. As I started to drive again, I received the call to confirm what I saw. He was able to respond in some fashion, and the doctors were more confident that his life would be spared. Hallelujah!

> [And besides this evidence] God also testifying with them [confirming the message of salvation], both by signs and wonders and by various miracles [carried out by Jesus and the apostles] and by [granting to believers the] gifts of the Holy Spirit according to His own will. (Hebrews 2:4 AMP)

Mindful

I ASKED THE FATHER TO HELP me lose weight and stop overeating just because the food tasted really good or because I was bored. I remembered date night several weeks in a row, and I continued to order salmon and broccoli. I said to myself...

ME. Wow! I only want salmon and broccoli again. I was planning to get something different.
GOD. Didn't you ask Me to help you lose weight?
ME. Yes, Lord. Thank You!

By then, I had forgotten what I asked of the Lord, but I'm so glad He didn't forget. Our God is so faithful!

What is man that You are mindful of him,
And the son of [earthborn] man that You care for
him? (Psalm 8:4 AMP)

Master

AFTER PREACHING THE WORD, MY conversation with the Lord went a little something like this.

GOD. I need you to cut your hair.
ME. Why, Lord?
GOD. You preached today, and the people were not listening to you.
ME. I thought they were really into what I was saying.
GOD. No, they were looking at your beautiful hair.
ME. Lord, that's not my fault. I didn't do anything wrong.

God led me to a scripture that talked about Paul becoming all things to all people so that he might win some. I realized I could not allow my hair to be a stumbling block to anyone's salvation or receiving the Word of the Lord.

> To the weak, I became [as the] weak, to win the weak. I have become all things to all men, so that I may by all means [in any and every way] save some [by leading them to faith in Jesus Christ]. (1 Corinthians 9:22 AMP)

God gave me a grace period. I cut more than half off, and then the barbershop was the last stop. I had been growing my hair, having fun with color and styles, and maintaining my locks for about ten years. I wasn't happy, but I was obedient.

> Samuel said, "Has the LORD as great a delight in burnt offerings and sacrifices as in obe-

dience to the voice of the LORD? Behold, to obey is better than sacrifice, and to heed [is better] than the fat of rams.

"For rebellion is as [serious as] the sin of divination (fortune-telling), and disobedience is as [serious as] false religion and idolatry. Because you have rejected the word of the LORD, He also has rejected you as king." (1 Samuel 15:22–23 AMP)

I didn't want to be rejected in my call and ministry. I want to fulfill all. Blessed be the name of the Lord!

Love

I was singing to the Lord while I washed dishes, and He interrupted me.

Me. Hallelujah! You have won the victory. Hallelujah! You have won it all for me.
God. Death couldn't stop Me from loving you. Death couldn't stop Me from pursuing you.
Me. Oh, God! (*crying real tears*)

He took my breath away. There I was, arrested with love and compassion like I've never known before. That day, Jesus captured my heart and my song all over again.

> For I am convinced [and continue to be convinced—beyond any doubt] that neither death, nor life, nor angels, nor principalities, nor things present and threatening, nor things to come, nor powers, nor height, nor depth, nor any other created thing, will be able to separate us from the [unlimited] love of God, which is in Christ Jesus our Lord. (Romans 8:38–39 AMP)

Living Water

One summer, my car broke down, and I bought an emergency minivan. It was old and ugly but drove well, and the brakes worked. There was no air conditioner, and this was one of the hottest summers we had in a long time. My son was about six months old, and I was busy in ministry and living in service for others.

Me. Lord, how are we going to get through this summer?
God. Courtesy cups of ice water.

That was it! Perfect for the baby cups, perfect for my sanity. I love the way He loves us.

> They will not hunger or thirst, Nor will the scorching heat or sun strike them down; For He who has compassion on them will lead them, And He will guide them to springs of water. (Isaiah 49:10 AMP)

Life

WE HAD A COWORKER WHO sustained a brain injury and was in a coma for weeks. Someone made a large "Get Well" board for her, and we were all going to write something on it.

FRIEND. We're taking the board to the hospital soon. Don't forget to write on it.
ME. I don't know what to write. I just want to tell her to get up.
FRIEND. Well, tell her to get up.
ME. Oh, okay.

I found a private spot at work and called out her name. Get up, get up, get up! Get up, get up, get up! Get up, get up, get up!

GOD. Now go get her a Bible and put her name on it.

After work, I picked out a Bible and put her name on it in gold letters. She was up and talking when I got there. She remembered me too. We talked, I sang to her, and massaged her feet. What a beautiful surprise. The next day at work, my friend was so sad talking about her.

ME. It's okay. She's up and talking now.
FRIEND. Since when?
ME. Yesterday. Remember you said, "Tell her to get up." Well, I told her to get up. God told me to get her a Bible, and when I got to the hospital, she was up. She is awake and talking as of yesterday.

Thank You, Jesus!

The thief comes only in order to steal and kill and destroy. I came that they may have life, and have it in abundance [to the full, till it overflows]. (John 10:10 AMP)

Life Support

The Lord gave me instructions concerning my teenage cousin. I had to take him to church with me and make sure he really understood and received the gift of salvation through our Lord and Savior Jesus Christ.

He was born again, baptized, and received what we call the *right hand of fellowship*, where people get in line to shake your hand, give money, speak blessings over your life, and welcome you into the body of Christ and/or the local church.

I drove thirty-five minutes both ways to pick him up and drop him back off at home. I had to minister to him along the way. We went through his room and threw away some things and then went into the backyard to burn some other things. I provided instruction, answered questions, prayed, read Scripture, and did anything and everything else the Lord requested of me. Over the span of three to four weeks, he was saved, growing, and walking in his new life in Christ. Praise the Lord!

About fifteen years later, I got a phone call that my cousin was in the hospital and on life support. When I saw him, my heart sank in. I know that God does all things well. He does things on purpose and with purpose, and He does not make mistakes.

Me. Father, I'm gonna need a return on my investment. You gave me instructions concerning this boy, and I did everything You told me to do. He cannot die like this. Please, Lord, not like this. I need a return on my investment, and I thank You for it all, in Jesus's name, amen.

God woke him up in not many days and brought him all the way through. He gave him another chance, and I will never forget it. Thank You, Father!

> Jesus said to her, "I am the Resurrection and the Life. Whoever believes in (adheres to, trusts in, relies on) Me [as Savior] will live even if he dies." (John 11:25 AMP)

Knowledge

Tʜᴇʀᴇ ᴡᴀs ᴀ ɢᴇɴᴛʟᴇᴍᴀɴ ɪɴᴛᴇʀᴇsᴛᴇᴅ in an exclusive relationship. As we talked and walked, the Lord showed me (in the spirit) three pieces of his paperwork. I saw a form DD-214 from the military, his birth certificate, and Social Security information. He said he had been divorced; however, I never saw the divorce decree within the paperwork that I saw in the spirit.

Mᴇ. I'm looking at your paperwork, and I don't see a divorce decree. Are you really divorced?
Hɪᴍ. What? You can see my paperwork? Yes, I'm divorced.
Mᴇ. Are you sure? I don't see a divorce decree.
Hɪᴍ. Well, I think so. I'll call my ex-wife and double-check.
Mᴇ. Okay.

A few days later, he found out they were not divorced, although they had been separated for over ten years. Nobody bothered to get a divorce. Praise the Lord! He won't allow us to miss anything. May you have eyes to see in the Spirit realm like never before, in Jesus's name, amen.

> The secret things belong to the Lᴏʀᴅ our God, but the things which are revealed and disclosed belong to us and to our children forever, so that we may do all of the words of this law. (Deuteronomy 29:29 AMP)

Justifier

I HAD A FRIEND SINCE NINTH grade, who decided in our forties that she was in love with my husband. She even tried to cause division to break us up. She went to great lengths to have him view me in a negative light. My phone was tapped, letters and emails were sent, and she even reached out to my family to talk about stuff I did in my twenties. Years later, I was speaking to an old friend and told him what transpired.

HIM. Oh, that's what the email was all about.
ME. What email?
HIM. I received an email years ago, talking about how she was trying to set you up. I still have it. Now I understand it, but I still don't know who sent it to me.

God will always keep one person around to validate your innocence. Learn to forgive quickly so God can be glorified in every dimension of your life. I am blessed as a married woman. I am blessed as a single woman. I will always be blessed because God does the blessing. When you belong to God, you always win. His words alone validate you and vindicate you.

> Who will bring any charge against God's
> elect (His chosen ones)? It is God who justifies us
> [declaring us blameless and putting us in a right
> relationship with Himself]. (Romans 8:33 AMP)

Justice

ONE SUMMER, I WAS HANGING out with my cousin and her children. I came home, and there was a lock on the basement door. I wanted to wash clothes, but I was no longer allowed to go into the basement. My mother thought I was taking food from our home to feed my cousin and her children.

ME. I am not a thief. I didn't take anything from this house and give it to anyone else.

MOM. Food is missing. I can't find it. It's not me nor your father, so it has to be you.

ME. I don't know where your food is, but I'm not a thief, and I'm not a liar.

Ten years later, God came all the way through for me. My father had passed away by then, and we were preparing to move out. As I was cleaning and throwing things away in the basement freezer, I found at least twenty pieces of chicken and steak, vacuum-packed and placed in a tall storage bucket. Three people ate that "stolen" meat for days. It was amazing because it was still good and fresh, after so many years. God restored my "good name" and the meat.

I don't ever remember getting an apology, but I sure do remember praising God for showing up. It doesn't matter how long it takes; God will still be around in ten years to show up for you. God echoed my words without saying a thing. I am not a liar, and I am not a thief.

Everything the enemy meant for bad in my life, God has always turned it around for my good. He always keeps someone around long enough to validate my innocence. No matter what! Whether little things, big things, in everything, I've learned to quickly forgive because God knows the truth and that's really all that matters.

Even if ten years have passed, may God show up to defend your good name. In Jesus's name, I pray, amen.

> The Lord judges the peoples;
> Judge me, O Lord, and grant me justice according to my righteousness and according to the integrity within me. (Psalm 7:8 AMP)

Judge

I had an issue and had to go to court.

Me. Father, please show me in a dream what's going to happen in the courtroom. Help me to be prepared, so I'll know exactly what to do and what to say.

God did it. He showed me the courtroom and everything that happened, through my dream. I stood there in awe because I could speak the words that were spoken even as the judge was speaking because I had already heard his words in my dream. However, I did not see the actual judgment. It was not in my favor. I was in court yet again, for the same type of incident two or three weeks later.

God. This time I will honor all of your requests.
Me. Thank You, Jesus!

And He certainly did.

> Beloved, never avenge yourselves, but leave the way open for God's wrath [and His judicial righteousness]; for it is written [in Scripture], "Vengeance is mine, I will repay," says the Lord. (Romans 12:19 AMP)

Joy

THE PASTOR PREACHED IN THE morning service and basically preached the same scriptures I had in mind for 4:00 p.m. He said many of the same words that I had in my notes. I went through fear, doubt, unbelief, and confusion. I was mad at God because I felt like it was a setup. After all, it was my initial message.

ME. Why would God do this to me? He knows all things so why would He allow this to happen to me? Why on the same day? Why now?

That day, God Himself had to speak to His own people. I had no words, and I was unprepared, but I am a worshipper so when the choir came forth to sing, I came forth too. The pastor looked as if to say, "It's okay, you don't have to sing tonight." I looked at him as if to say, "Oh yes, I do." I got lost in praise and worship and forgot I had nothing to preach.

The Holy Spirit took over and brought to my remembrance all the necessary things I had already studied. Who needs notes, right? He even reminded me of a vision I had of that very day.

I described a day to my pastor, about eighteen months prior. I remembered the scene, but I didn't know what the occasion was. I told him I had on black and described how the church was situated and sectioned off. I had never seen it like that before, and I didn't know what we were celebrating, but I was behind the podium. That was normal. Because I'm a psalmist and soloist, it was likely for me to be at the podium, behind the microphone.

We soon found out that everything that happened that day was purposeful and preordained by God. He wanted to show me and the congregation that this was our moment in Him, that He's mindful of us, and that He really is in control. It was miraculous! It was a blessing, and when the Holy Spirit was done, I was done. Hallelujah! Sweaty and out of breath, all I could think to say was *Hallelujah*! I cannot put into words all the emotions involved with that experience. Several *God things* happened that day. His people were blessed, and I was lost in His presence.

> You will show me the path of life; In Your presence is fullness of joy; In Your right hand, there are pleasures forevermore. (Psalm 16:11 AMP)

Jehovah Sabaoth, the Lord of Hosts

My sister almost drowned in a pool. She was walking down the stairs and missed the last step. I looked down and saw her gasping for air. She tried to hold onto the side of the pool and chipped her tooth. I saw blood in the water, and I was so afraid. I screamed asking anybody and everybody for help, but ended up pulling my sister out of the water myself.

We still don't know how I got her out of the water. I was about nine years old, which makes her around twelve years old and probably twice my weight. God must've had an angel pulling with me. It makes no natural sense that I was able to pull her out of the water on my own.

But God!

> For He will command His angels in regard to you, To protect and defend and guard you in all your ways [of obedience and service]. (Psalm 91:11 AMP)

Jealous

I COOKED DINNER FOR MY SIGNIFICANT other. He loved vegetables, and I went out of my way to cut his veggies perfectly. I laid them out in the pan in a beautiful, colorful pattern. I wanted him to know and see that I cared about the presentation of his meal. I was really into making a great dinner. I wanted things to be perfect for him. I was excited to have him over for dinner for the first time in my new apartment.

ME. Yes, that's it. This looks so nice.
GOD. Yes, it does, and you'd better take your time to prepare My
     meal the next time you preach that word.
ME. (*Gasp!*)

I felt like a deer caught in headlights. Suddenly, the dinner wasn't so exciting. I felt like I was in idolatry, like I was cheating on Jesus. I couldn't believe He was really watching me go through all those emotions about fixing a man's dinner to the point where He was offended.

I repented immediately. That ended up being one of the shortest dinners we've ever had. I felt like God was watching us eat. That actually may have been our last dinner. I had to get myself together and redirect all of my attention to God right away.

ME. I don't understand Your great love for me.
GOD. You don't have to understand it. You just have to accept it.
ME. I accept it.

I am jealous for you with a godly jealousy
because I have promised you to one husband, to

present you as a pure virgin to Christ. But I am afraid that, even as the serpent beguiled Eve by his cunning, your minds may be corrupted and led away from the simplicity of [your sincere and] pure devotion to Christ. (2 Corinthians 11:2–3 AMP)

I Am

God had given me a promise, but this special promise was also going to be my surprise. I am nosy when it comes to the things of God because we have been talking (it feels like) all my life. He answers my prayers, plays with me, and tells me jokes. Yes, jokes! I Am is hilarious when you get to know Him. He had been giving me numbers, symbols, hints, and music to encourage me along the way. I still had to do my part to prepare and make ready to receive my promise/surprise.

Me. Oh, I Am, thank You so much. I had an amazing dream. In the dream, I received my surprise, and it felt so real. I was so happy.

It's coming, I Am. You're doing this. As I'm driving down the road, thinking about our conversation, I'm getting kind of antsy.

Me. I want my promise, I want my reward, and I want my surprise. You can't lie, You can't fail, and all things are possible for You to do. So please, manifest my surprise and my reward because I'm ready.

I see numbers 5-3-2-1 on a license plate. The plate caught my attention because it also included my initials. He knew, of course, that I was going to see it.

Me. No more signs and symbols, please, no more numbers. I'm ready for the manifestation of what You spoke to me. Please just manifest my surprise and my reward because I'm ready. Please, no more. Just do what You said You were going to do!

Meanwhile, I was working with a client who had been in pain for weeks. Doctors and medication did not help. After our session, she was pain-free, dancing, twisting, and praising God. She gave me hugs and kisses, and we blessed the Lord for coming through.

Now I was praising the Lord for her breakthrough and for using me in such a supernatural way. On the way home (still praising), He reminded me of the things I said and my attitude regarding His Word. I quickly repented. I confessed and asked for forgiveness for what I said and for my attitude.

ME. Please forgive me, I Am, and thank You for continuing to come through for us over and over again. I repent for my attitude. I'm sorry. Thank You for using me, for speaking to me, and encouraging me along the way.

I said all the things to clear my head, stay out of trouble, and get back in line with the will of God.

ME. I Am, what is the number for manifestation anyway? Is there a number in Greek that means manifestation?

Wouldn't you know it? *5-3-2-1 phanerosis*: a manifestation from the Greek *Strong's Concordance*.

Right? It's not funny. Okay, yes, it is funny. Can you imagine? I felt like a *first-class heel* (for all *The Flintstone* fans). He is not to be played with. I Am can do whatever He wants to do, however and whenever He wants to do it. He can have His way with me. I'm done!

> God said to Moses, "I AM WHO I AM"; and
> He said, "You shall say this to the Israelites, 'I
> AM has sent me to you.'" (Exodus 3:14 AMP)

As I looked up the scripture for this encounter, I Am reminded me that my son (the one where I Am requested my womb) was born at 3:14 am.
Song: "Didn't I (Blow Your Mind This Time)" By The Delfonics
Then I serenaded Him with "Weak" by SWV.

I came into the house to read this to my son, and he reminded me that when he was little, he didn't like the number 4. He would say, "One, two, three, five."

Husband

Aﬁᴛᴇʀ ᴍʏ ᴅɪᴠᴏʀᴄᴇ, I ᴛʀɪᴇᴅ to pawn my engagement ring, sell it, whatever. No one was interested in my ring. I think it's beautiful and different, and apparently, it was all mine.

Gᴏᴅ. He gave you that ring, but it's from Me.
Mᴇ. Oh, Lord, I'm sorry. You're right. We talked about this ring before he even came along. Thank You.

I had loved the ring from afar for about one year. It was like God set it right there for me. I declared ownership of that ring, and I knew it was mine right away.

Mᴇ. Oh, Lord, it's flawed!
Gᴏᴅ. So are you.

He captured my heart once again, right at the jewelry counter. I laughed and cried tears of joy as I worshipped the love of my life, my First Love.

> For your husband is your Maker, The Lᴏʀᴅ of hosts is His name; And your Redeemer is the Holy One of Israel, Who is called the God of the whole earth. (Isaiah 54:5 AMP)

Hiding Place

I WAS FASTING FOR THE FIRST time for forty days with no food. We were having testimony time in church, and that Sunday happened to be day 37 of my fast.

DEVIL. God is not going to bless you. You should go ahead and eat.
ME. You are stupid. Where have you been? Don't you know this is day 37?

I laughed so hard, I don't even remember rebuking him. I shared that with my pastor, and we were so happy and gave God the glory. I laughed at the devil. His expectation over my life will never be met in Jesus's name. I was hidden from the enemy for thirty-seven days. Hallelujah!

> You are my hiding place; You, LORD, protect
> me from trouble; You surround me with songs
> and shouts of deliverance. (Psalm 32:7 AMP)

It still amazes me how I can look at a calendar and see that I haven't eaten in twenty-one, twenty-eight, or thirty-five days and not be hungry. God is so amazing! I have friends who still ask me how can I do that.

ME. It's not me. It's the God within me.

I cannot take credit for something I don't fully understand. I do know it's a powerful tool that has broken addiction, thought patterns, and cycles, health and bloodline issues, and more of me and my family. I read the word, pray, worship, and try my best to block out distractions so I can hear and obey. I sow seeds (tithes, offerings) and thank God in advance for harvests of all kinds. I meditate on the Word of God and claim all the promises attached to the fast that God has chosen from Isaiah 58:6–14:

> [Rather] is this not the fast which I choose, To undo the bonds of wickedness, To tear to pieces the ropes of the yoke, To let the oppressed go free And break apart every [enslaving] yoke? Is it not to divide your bread with the hungry And bring the homeless poor into the house; When you see the naked, that you cover him, And not to hide yourself from [the needs of] your own flesh and blood? Then your light will break out like the dawn, And your healing (restoration, new life) will quickly spring forth; Your righteousness will go before you [leading you to peace and prosperity], The glory of the LORD will be your rear guard. Then you will call, and the LORD will answer; You will cry for help, and He will say, "Here I am." If you take away from your midst the yoke [of oppression], The finger pointed in scorn [toward the oppressed or the godly], and [every form of] wicked (sinful, unjust) speech, And if you offer yourself to [assist] the hungry And satisfy the need of the afflicted, Then your light will rise in darkness And your gloom will become like midday. And the LORD will continually guide you, And satisfy your soul in scorched and dry places, And give strength to your bones; And you will be like a watered garden, And like a spring of water whose waters do not fail. And your people will rebuild the ancient ruins; You will raise up and restore the age-old foundations [of buildings that have been laid waste]; You

will be called Repairer of the Breach, Restorer of Streets with Dwellings. "If you turn back your foot from [unnecessary travel on] the Sabbath, From doing your own pleasure on My holy day, And call the Sabbath a [spiritual] delight, and the holy day of the LORD honorable, And honor it, not going your own way Or engaging in your own pleasure Or speaking your own [idle] words, Then you will take pleasure in the LORD, And I will make you ride on the high places of the earth, And I will feed you with the [promised] heritage of Jacob your father; For the mouth of the LORD has spoken."

Amen.

Heavy

My three-year-old and I were lying in bed, talking in the dark. Suddenly, he stopped talking to me and seemed to be falling asleep. I called out to him.

Me. Son, are you asleep?
Son. Shhh, Mommy. I'm praying.
Me. (Thinking, did he just shush me?) Oh, okay.

Two minutes later…

Me. Hey, are you asleep?
Son. Shhh, Mommy. I'm praying.
Me. Oh, okay. (*thinking, Did he just shush me again?*)

Two minutes later…

Me. Hey, son, are you asleep?
Son. (*Crying*) Mommy, can you see him? Heavy is here! Mommy, can you see him?
Me. No, son. Who is "Heavy?"
Son. Mommy, can you see him? Heavy! Heavy is here!
Me. No, son. I can't see him. Are you okay?
Son. Yes, Mommy. He's gone now.

I was disturbed and confused, but God quickly told me to look up the word *heavy*. "Heavy" means *kabed* or *kavod* in Hebrew. The Hebrew word *kavod* originally meant heavy, weighty, as in reference to armor used in battle. Over time, the word became linked with wealth, honor, dignity, and power, and it eventually came to mean "glory." All these attributes combine to describe God as El Hakkavod, "The God of Glory." Hallelujah! I was so happy. I invited "Heavy" to come and visit us anytime.

> For God, who said, "Let light shine out of
> darkness," is the One who has shone in our hearts
> to give us the Light of the knowledge of the glory
> and majesty of God [clearly revealed] in the face
> of Christ. (2 Corinthians 4:6 AMP)

Heavenly Father

My sons are almost twenty-one years apart. My older son saw his baby brother at birth and then about six months later. He thought his baby brother didn't know him anymore and asked him for a hug when it was time to go.

Son. Ma, he doesn't even remember me.
Me. I'm sure he knows you're his brother.

My older son reached out, and the baby looked back at me.

Son. See, Ma, he doesn't even know me.

The baby took his pacifier out of his mouth and started to put it in his brother's mouth.

Me. (*Laughing*) See, he remembers you. He's never shared his pacifier with me.

> Little children (believers, dear ones), let us not love [merely in theory] with word or with tongue [giving lip service to compassion], but in action and in truth [in practice and in sincerity, because practical acts of love are more than words]. (1 John 3:18 AMP)

Healer

MY SON HAD CHICKEN POX worse than the cousins he con-
tracted it from. I bought everything I could buy for his comfort. Yet
he continued to cry and scream, helplessly in the corner. I cried with
him. There was no more that I could do. I told him the next time he
screams, scream, "Jesus!"

SON. Jesus! Jesus! Jesus! Jesus! Jesus! Jesus! Jesus!
SON. Hey, Ma. The pain and the itching are gone.
ME. Well, Hallelujah! Tell the Lord, "Thank You!"
SON. Thank You, Lord.

My Healer became my son's Healer right before my eyes. Glory
to the Lamb of God!

> We will not hide them from their children,
> But [we will] tell to the generation to come the
> praiseworthy deeds of the Lord, And [tell of] His
> great might and power and the wonderful works
> that He has done. (Psalm 78:4 AMP)

Gracious

MY YOUNGEST SON WAS MY birthday present.

ME. Please don't let me give birth at forty. Please don't let me give birth at forty.

My son came three days before my birthday. I had a healthy, happy ball of light. I dedicated every contraction to Jesus because this child was His idea. He was most gracious and answered my prayer. We celebrate the whole month by trying to do, eat, or learn something different every day.

> The LORD is gracious and full of compassion, slow to anger and abounding in lovingkindness. (Psalm 145:8 AMP)

Good

AFTER MASSAGING MY CLIENT, I asked if she would like to add a gratuity for her session.

CLIENT. Yes.
ME. Okay, thank you! How much?
CLIENT. $750.
ME. Excuse me?
CLIENT. $750.
ME. Are you sure?
CLIENT. Yes, I want to bless you!
ME. Well, thank you. Thank you very much. Praise the Lord!

It was the biggest tip I had ever received (so far), and I really needed it. God has sent many people over the years to sow into my life and business right on time. What God has done for others, He can certainly do for you. Prepare for great harvests because God will reward your faithfulness. Our God will never fail.

> Now He who provides seed for the sower and bread for food will provide and multiply your seed for sowing [that is, your resources] and increase the harvest of your righteousness [which shows itself in active goodness, kindness, and love]. (2 Corinthians 9:10 AMP)

God

I WAS WALKING ALONG, GETTING THINGS done in my home when the Lord spoke.

GOD. Get on your face.

I stopped and immediately got down on my face. It's a normal position of prayer for me, but this time I felt painful lumps in my left breast. I continued to pray and rebuke whatever was trying to take up residence in my breast and in my body.

While in prayer, the lumps started to break up and dissolve until I was no longer in pain. My prayers quickly turned into praise. Although the Lord could've healed me any other way, I thank God for the willingness to be obedient.

> Behold, I am the LORD, the God of all flesh;
> is there anything too difficult for Me? (Jeremiah
> 32:27 AMP)

God with a Plan

I STARTED A NONPROFIT ORGANIZATION AND met with someone to assist me with the application process and all the things I needed to do to make sure that I was in compliance with government regulations. When the time came to apply for nonprofit status, the mentor/ help was no longer available. I quickly found myself in my feelings, feeling rejected once again, and challenged the Lord:

ME. Did You not give this to me?
GOD. Do the application yourself.
ME. Lord, I've never done anything like this before, and I don't want to make any mistakes.
GOD. I will help you.
ME. Okay, Lord, thank You. I'll do it.

I grabbed my computer and started reading all the information to make sure my *vision* qualified as a nonprofit, where to put information, including who will be on the board, and all the other necessary information. I finally got to the payment screen and noticed that the application was $275. I was told that it was $400, and I was prepared to pay the $400. I feared that after all the entries I had made, I had pulled up the wrong application. I called the IRS to explain my situation, and the representative said, that as of July 1 of that year, the nonprofit application had decreased by $125. Hallelujah! Glory to God!

After having been in my feelings and reluctantly doing the application by myself, I realized that had I received the help when I planned to do the application, I would have paid $400. God came all the way through for me and treated me to a spa day with the $125. Thank You, Daddy! Glory!

> "For I know the plans and thoughts that I have for you," says the Lord, "plans for peace and well-being and not for disaster, to give you a future and a hope." (Jeremiah 29:11 AMP)

God of My Process

I HAD TORN MY ROTATOR CUFF muscle on the right side. I heard and felt the tear as I was doing a chair massage.

ME. Oh no! (*in my mind*)
GOD. Yep. It's torn.

I was able to continue my day and press through the discomfort and pain. My neck and shoulder started to swell, and when I got home, the conversation went something like this.

ME. Okay, Father! Who's going to heal this, me or You?
GOD. You are. You did it.
ME. Okay. What do I need to do?

God had already provided everything I needed for muscle repair and rebuilding.

1. He told me, two weeks prior, to buy collagen for my coffee.
2. He had a client bless me with a bottle of complete amino.
3. I had already purchased barley grass for weight management and detox, and
4. He already had me eating a high-protein diet.

All these things were already within arm's reach when the tear happened. I found myself reading and rereading labels because I couldn't believe Him.

GOD. Now get the tape.

Me. The tape, where is it?

He led me directly to the KT tape. I had not taken a class to properly tape minor injuries. So the picture on the box had a lady with her arm taped in the same place as my injury. Yay, Daddy Jesus!
I have been working the whole time, with a modified schedule, and He has done marvelous things. Praise the Lord!

> But He knows the way that I take [and He pays attention to it]. *When* He has tried me, I will come forth as [refined] gold [pure and luminous]. (Job 23:10 AMP)

God of All Flesh

I WAS HAVING A CONVERSATION WITH my coworker about what we were going to do after returning to work from Christmas break.

GOD. You will not be returning to work.
ME. Where am I going, Jesus?
GOD. You're going to school.
ME. What school am I going to, Jesus?
GOD. Esthetics school.

I told Him all the reasons I couldn't go to school. I even wrote a very thorough list of everything I needed to make it happen. God worked it all out; He gave me directions and instructions. He even sent me a weekend babysitter, a Sunday school teacher who took my son to church with her. Hallelujah!

I enrolled, and there was an interesting question at the end of the application.

Question: If you think about quitting school, what can we say to you to encourage you to finish the course?

Answer: Remember who sent you here.

I would constantly remind myself, "My Father sent me here, and I'll see you at graduation."

I went to school full-time and launched my new business. I worked seven days a week. Home, child care, school, office, and weekend child care were all within ten minutes of one another. My school and office were even a block away.

I was on academic probation, financial probation, and attendance probation. I became acquainted with the dean and all the business offices. My friends were concerned for me, but I kept smiling.

Me. I'll be right back.
Friends. Are you sure this time?
Me. My Father sent me here, and I'll see you at graduation.

I had a great favor. I even asked my massage clients to come over to the school. I would see them after hours and upgrade their packages to include a free facial. The administrators allowed me to get all my hours in, just in time. I remember being so exhausted. I didn't even make it to graduation, but I finished my course. Hallelujah!

Me. You did it, Lord. I didn't think it was possible.

> Behold, I am the Lord, the God of all flesh;
> is there anything too difficult for Me? (Jeremiah
> 32:27 AMP)

Giver

I CUT MY LIP ON A soup spoon at one of my favorite restaurants. Everyone was very kind, and I took pictures of my lip as it was swelling. I was able to continue eating, so I wasn't really alarmed, but I wanted to know what the procedure was for something like this.

The manager took my information and gave me a gift card (I used it that day), and her business card. Someone from the corporate office would contact me within two to three days to check on me and see how things went.

Corporate was very nice. I gave my server an excellent review and let them know all was well. My lip was fine. The swelling must have come from the spices in the food as the skin had just been broken. I was to receive a gift card through email for my inconvenience, and that was fine for me. I ended up getting two gift cards for a substantial amount. That was amazing to me and right on time. My God blessed me with extra, He gave me double for my trouble.

> Instead of your [former] shame *you will have* a double portion; And *instead of* humiliation your people will shout for joy over their *portion*. Therefore in their land they will possess double [what they had forfeited]; Everlasting joy will be theirs. (Isaiah 61:7 AMP)

Friend

I was bragging to God about our relationship and thanking Him for always coming through for me and putting things within arm's reach. Shortly afterward, someone asked me for my business card. I didn't have one on me, and my purse was in the car.

I just smiled at Him. I loved it. It was like God was saying, "Psych!" (Please excuse me. I'm from Baltimore.)

He's my everything!

He gave me an opportunity to go to my car and grab a business card after He "psyched" me.

> The man of *too many friends* [chosen indiscriminately] will be broken in pieces *and* come to ruin, But there is a [true, loving] friend who [is reliable and] sticks closer than a brother. (Proverbs 18:24 AMP)

Forgiveness

MY COWORKERS AND I HAD several disagreements. Words were exchanged, and I ended up being terminated from my job. I was talked about so badly by many of them, but by one lady in particular. Some things I knew about and some things were revealed later. Either way, no one could ever deny God's hand upon my life.

About two weeks after my departure, the lady (who had much to say) had her baby. The baby was diagnosed with a hole in his heart. She called me and asked me to pray for him; she apologized for all the things she said about me and proceeded to tell me what the doctors had to say.

ME. I forgive you. All is well. Let us pray!

After we prayed, I told her her son was going to be fine, and just call me with the good report. She called me back in not many days. Somehow, the hole repaired itself and the baby was able to go home soon.

Hallelujah! God came through for her baby boy!

> Therefore, confess your sins to one another [your false steps, your offenses], and pray for one another, that you may be healed and restored. The heartfelt and persistent prayer of a righteous man (believer) is able to accomplish much [when put into action and made effective by God—it is dynamic and can have tremendous power]. (James 5:16 AMP)

Faithful

I HAD GONE TO THE MALL and discovered a new store that had a lot of items for relaxation. I went in to browse, and the sales lady offered me the chance to lay on the couch for three minutes and have a lavender beanbag on my forehead. She instructed me to just close my eyes, drift away, and just receive whatever beauty comes to my mind.

I took her up on her offer; I worked a lot, so I needed to relax. There I lay with the lavender bag on my forehead. I did drift away as expected, but what I saw was unexpected as I drifted off to sleep. When she woke me up after about what felt like fifteen minutes, she asked how my rest was.

ME. Wonderful. I feel great, refreshed.
LADY. Where did you go? Can you share? What did you see?
ME. I was dancing for the Lord, in my church. It was so beautiful, very colorful, and dramatic.
LADY. Oh, that sounds lovely.
ME. It was, but I don't dance. I sing.

Many years later, God had a pastor prophesy to me. I had never met her. She stood in my face and told me I had to dance before the Lord.

PASTOR. And when you dance, the Glory of the Lord will fill the atmosphere, and deliverance will take place.

I made the commitment to dance for the Lord on Mother's Day. The glory fell, deliverance took place, and God changed the order of the whole service.

Hallelujah!

> I am convinced *and* confident of this very thing, that He who has begun a good work in you will [continue to] perfect *and* complete it until the day of Christ Jesus [the time of His return]. (Philippians 1:6 AMP)

El Kano, Jealous

In college, I had two close friends, and we would cheer loud and hard for our football team. One time, we won money, $50 each, for being the loudest group. Some said we could actually be heard on the opposite side of the football field. We loved it.

When I came back home and started going to church again, the Lord said…

God. I need more from you. You can't scream louder for the football team than you scream for Me.

Me. Wow, God! Okay, yes, sir.

He's even called me out publicly. If God feels like I'm holding back, He will have visiting prophets call me out. I'm always the loudest one in church. In the beginning, I was very self-conscious and aware of people's reactions. I hear the (not-so-quiet) whispers, "It doesn't take all that," "She doesn't have to be so loud," and "God's not deaf."

That's my favorite one. Yet none of it has ever been worth my response. I'm just now sharing publicly why I'm so loud during praise and worship.

Jesus is Lord! It's in Him that we live and move and have our being. He's going to get everything He requires out of me, without apology!

> From everyone to whom much has been given, much will be required; and to whom they entrusted much, of him they will ask all the more.
> (Luke 12:48b AMP)

Dream Giver

I HAD A DREAM THAT I bought a car. I got all my paperwork together and went to the dealership. I told the lady my situation and what money I had.

LADY. You need to see Mike.
ME. Okay, where is he?

I went to another dealership and asked for Mike. I waited for about an hour, and then Mike came in, looking like he had just finished vacation. About an hour later, my paperwork was approved. It turns out Mike was the owner of a very popular chain of dealerships in our area. God led me to the answer, but it started with a dream.

> And He said, "Hear my words: If there is
> a prophet among you, I, the Lord, make myself
> known to him in a vision; I speak with him in a
> dream." (Numbers 12:6 AMP)

Director

I HAD ERRANDS TO RUN AND asked the Lord to remind me of all I had to do. I had done a few things and was on my way home.

GOD. Dollar store.
ME. Thank You, Lord.

I was approaching a red light and slowly moved into the left lane to make a left turn for the dollar store. Before the light turned green, the car that took my place was hit by an oncoming car, which was cut off by a turning vehicle.

That would've been me, had God not reminded me to go to the dollar store. Several people called the police. The driver who failed to make the turn successfully ran to my car. She was frantic and didn't even see the other car. It all happened so fast. I tried to calm her down and just quietly prayed over the situation.

Off I went, after the cars were moved, recapping the incident and praising God. He moved me to avoid a bad accident. I prayed for those involved, of course, but I'm thankful for my relationship with the Father through Jesus Christ. He was faithful to remind me, and I bless the Lord for my obedience.

> God, having spoken to the fathers long ago
> in [the voices and writings of] the prophets in
> many separate revelations [each of which set forth
> a portion of the truth], and in many ways, has in
> these last days spoken [with finality] to us in [the
> person of One who is by His character and nature]
> His Son [namely Jesus]. (Hebrews 1:1–2a AMP)

Daddy

I was just talking out loud one day.

Me. Daddy, I want a sunroof.

The next day, the car dealer called me to let me know that the company was doing their own financing and to come and pick out a new car. I could have a brand-new vehicle with more upgrades plus save about 75 percent of my current interest.

Me. Thank you, Daddy! Can I also have leather seats and a remote start?

I was nervous at first, but I serve the exceeding abundant God. He reminded me of what He said years ago.

God. I own all the dealerships. You will drive the car I need you to drive for the season.
Me. Amen.

My car was less than two years old, yet I left out with both keys, title, and insurance paperwork in hand, asking my Daddy to pick out the perfect new car for us. Glory! It's perfect for us. It's the top-of-the-line model, with four miles on it when I got in. Thank You, Daddy! It's everything I asked for and so much more.

Salesman. It doesn't happen often where I can really see a blessing. I wasn't sure about it when you told me all you wanted. I was

going to just do my best. But when my manager said we can do this, I was so happy for you. Thank God!
ME. Amen. Thank God.

> Delight yourself in the LORD, And He will
> give you the desires and petitions of your heart.
> (Psalm 37:4 AMP)

Creator

I WANTED TO GET TO A stream, reservoir, or some natural, moving water. My friends found a beautiful place where we could relax, enjoy the environment, and pray. I walked off to be alone. I just needed to know that God was there after all; He felt so far away.

ME. Lord, please give me a sign or something. I just really need to know You are with me. Lord, can you make a big fish jump out of the water so I can see him make a big splash?

A turtle walked over.

ME. Thank You, Mr. Turtle, but you're not quite what I'm looking for.

I got bit by a few mosquitoes but still wasn't convinced of God's presence. I didn't go all the way to the water to get bitten by mosquitoes. I could have stayed in the city for that. Then a big fish jumped out of the water and made a loud splash. That was Him!

ME: Thank you, Lord. Thank you, Mr. Fish. That was just what I needed and what I asked for.

I felt empowered, and strengthened, like I wasn't alone, and I knew my prayers were being heard. I know I should've just had faith, but I didn't, and I'm so glad that God met me right where I was.

If any of you lacks wisdom [to guide him
through a decision or circumstance], he is to ask

of [our benevolent] God, who gives to everyone
generously and without rebuke *or* blame, and it
will be given to him. (James 1:5 AMP)

Compassionate

My father knows that I love when things are within arm's reach. I am spoiled when it comes to my Jesus. He makes me feel like I'm His favorite. I really do expect Him to give me the desires of my heart no matter how big, small, or petty. He's my Daddy, and He knows that there's something special about things being within *arm's reach* for me.

I believe I've been so busy for so long that I really haven't been granted extra time to look for things. With my life, that would just seem like just one more thing to do. My daddy knows where everything is, everything! So I depend on Him to put things within arm's reach.

He has been so amazing with *arm's reach* these days. One day in particular, I was at work and had a really bad issue with a bulging disc in my lower back and radiating nerve pain. The only thing that I found that works for nerve pain was peppermint oil. I happened to look in my purse and there was my peppermint oil. I had not seen it for weeks, if not months, because I didn't need it. I actually prefer Spearmint Essential Oil to diffuse in my home and in my car, so I was totally unaware that the peppermint oil was in my purse.

God knew! I just smiled at Him. He knew I had no idea. I felt like He put it in my purse before I left the house. He led me to look in my purse, and to my surprise, there it was. I was able to calm the fire of nerve pain and finish my work shift. Glory to God!

Jesus tells me a lot of things, but when He's not speaking, He has the best surprises. Hallelujah!

> It is because of the Lord's lovingkindnesses
> that we are not consumed, Because His [ten-

der] compassions never fail. They are new every morning; *Great and beyond* measure is Your faithfulness. (Lamentations 3:22–23 AMP)

Comfort

THERE WAS A FORECAST OF a terrible tropical storm moving into our area. I started reading the details about the storm from the cell phone alert. Where was it coming from, how fast was the wind, and what was the expected damage? It was as if God was looking over my shoulder at what I was doing. I started praying the opposite of the forecast, line by line.

GOD. Just pluck the eye out of the storm.
ME. Oh, okay.

I plucked the eye out of the storm in Jesus's name and went on my way. I had so much comfort and peace. I had forgotten about it, but someone happened to mention it during our prayer call. The tropical storm that was expected ended up being a fall rain, pleasant and cool. I received the word of the Lord, so it was up to Him to fulfill His own word and make it happen.

We pray and intercede the best we know how, but it's nothing like participating with the Lord and watching Him work. God's word will never return void.

Hallelujah!

> So will My word be which goes out of My mouth; It will not return to Me void (useless, without result), without accomplishing what I desire, and without succeeding in the matter for which I sent it. (Isaiah 55:11 AMP)

Chiropractor

I NEEDED TO GET TO THE bottom of my healing, or lack thereof. I know that the devil has no access to my body. I know that healing and deliverance are the children's bread. So I had to get with the Holy Spirit, my Counselor, to find out why I was diagnosed with a bulging disc, why the random pain, and why I couldn't feel the last three toes on my left foot. Enough is enough!

GOD. (*hours later*) Don't forget to get on your face.
ME. You're the only One who can get me down here because I know You can get me back up.

I got interrupted and got off the floor. I did a few things in my room.

GOD. Don't forget to get on your face.
ME. Amen.

I prepared my way of worship and lay on my face, just praising and thanking God. I didn't really forget to ask about my healing, but I was just happy to be in His presence. Because of the pain, it had been a while since I had been on my face. After about ten minutes or so, my lower back shook involuntarily, I rocked my hips back and forth then came up on my knees with no pain whatsoever.

ME. Thank You, Lord, for my healing, and forgive me for taking so long to get down here.

It felt like a chiropractic adjustment, but I received my permanent healing, in Jesus's name.

> Heal me, O Lord, and I will be healed; save me and I will be saved, for You are my praise. (Jeremiah 17:14 AMP)

Chef

Jesus has taught me to prepare many dishes, and He helps me tweak the recipes to make them my own. I've become quite creative with vegetables, crab, and cereals. Websites are awesome, but cooking with Jesus is so much fun. I don't really like to follow directions and recipes, but I love when He tells me to put more of this and less of that. He even reminds me that after long fasts, I don't have the same tastes for certain foods that I used to have.

I no longer desire sweeteners in my coffee and tea, I rarely use spices in my food, and my air fryer helps me to stay away from certain oils. I am so satisfied now, eating at home, and I don't feel like I'm missing out on anything. I know exactly what's in my food and how it was prepared. He helped me make an awesome crab imperial (one of my favs), and I'm no longer desiring the restaurant's style. I don't want sugar in all my food. My constant prayer is for health, strength, and long life. With Chef Jesus, I am well on my way.

> Trust in and rely confidently on the Lord with all your heart and do not rely on your own insight or understanding. In all your ways, know and acknowledge and recognize Him, and He will make your paths straight and smooth [removing obstacles that block your way]. Do not be wise in your own eyes; fear the Lord [with reverent awe and obedience] and turn [entirely] away from evil. It will be health to your body [your marrow, your nerves, your sinews, your muscles—all your inner parts] and refreshment (physical well-being) to your bones. (Proverbs 3:5–8 AMP)

Caring

I RENTED A BASEMENT APARTMENT FOR a year that was pretty much fully furnished. We enjoyed a sixty-inch TV with surround sound and cable. When it was time to move, I realized I had gotten spoiled with the sixty-inch TV. One of my regular clients was downsizing and wanted to sell a sixty-inch TV with a glass TV stand and three shelves. Coincidence? Not when my Daddy knows I wanted a sixty-inch TV.

ME. Beautiful. I'll take it.

We bartered 25 percent of the cash and the balance in massage sessions.

> As for the rich in this present world, instruct them not to be conceited and arrogant, nor to set their hope on the uncertainty of riches, but on God, who richly and ceaselessly provides us with everything for our enjoyment. (1 Timothy 6:17 AMP)

Boss

I WAS RECOVERING FROM SURGERY AND needed a new job, a desk job. I interviewed with a dentist for the front office manager and thought the interview went well. He took about ten days to two weeks to follow up with me. By then I was beginning to get discouraged. Much to my surprise, as I was praying and waiting, God was speaking to him on my behalf. Our conversation went a little something like this...

DENTIST. God told me to hire you, but He said you would not be with me for a long time.
ME. Really? Thank you. Did He say where I was going next?
DENTIST. No.

I was there for about three years. I enrolled in a massage therapy school and had night classes until I graduated and obtained my license to practice. I took myself to lunch after an interview and God spoke to me.

GOD. When do you want to leave the office?
ME. October 31.
GOD. Okay.

I gave notice to my employer that the time had come for me to leave. I hired my replacement and was off to a new start with God. I was hired right away as a massage therapist and found an office to start my own practice as well.

My employer originally wanted someone who would be there
more than three years, but I'm thankful that God spoke on my behalf.
I'm also thankful for His obedience.

Hallelujah!

> For it is [not your strength, but it is] God
> who is effectively at work in you, both to will
> and to work [that is, strengthening, energizing,
> and creating in you the longing and the ability
> to fulfill your purpose] for His good pleasure.
> (Philippians 2:13 AMP)

Blesser

GOD ASKED ME TO DO a forty-day fast with no food.

ME. No, Lord, that's for You and Moses. I can't do that.
GOD. I need you to do this fast.
ME. Can't you get somebody else to do it?
GOD. I could, but I'm trying to bless you.
ME. Okay. (*reluctantly*)

I was preparing to start on January 1, yet He spoke again.

GOD. What would you like for your Christmas dinner?
ME. Chicken, meatballs, and snow crab legs.
GOD. Okay, you can have that.

As I finished Christmas dinner…

GOD. How do you like your food?
ME. Everything is so good. Thank You, Lord.
GOD. Good! I need you to start the fast tomorrow.
ME. Tomorrow?
GOD. You heard what I said, and wherever you look for confirmation, you'll find it.
ME. Okay. Well, You always do things on purpose, so if You want me to start on the 26th, let me see what the number 26 means.

I looked up the number 26 in English and Hebrew, which means the name of the God of Israel (*Yahovah*) in Hebrew. I just started praising the Lord in awe, excitement, and unbelief all at the same time.

Me. Okay, Lord, one more!
God. Okay.

I counted through the forty days, and the last day would be February 4. This means I could eat for my son's birthday and my birthday. Had I started the fast on January 1, I would not have been able to eat on either of our birthdays. Hallelujah!

Me. What? I'm done. I'm done. I'm done. I'm in. (*Screaming*)

I will surely bless you and I will surely multiply you. (Hebrews 6:14 AMP)

Best Friend

THE NIGHT I RECEIVED PROOF of infidelity, I put on jeans and Timberland boots. I told God I was going to go kick her teeth out of her mouth. I sat in my car and called my pastor in case I went to jail. I told her I might need her to bail me out and/or to let her know why I wouldn't be in service on Sunday.

ME. I'm going to kick her teeth out of her mouth.
PASTOR. Don't do that. Do not go over there.
ME. Love you. Bye.

I knocked on the door. She knew who I was and opened the front door right away. When she opened her screen door and spoke, I realized she had no teeth in the front of her mouth. I was so disappointed.

ME. (*In my mind*) Dang, Lord! I can't even kick her teeth out.

God took hold of me that I will never forget. I walked through that door with a smile on my face because I was laughing on the inside. I wasn't even mad anymore. It was like a sour joke played on me by my best friend. How could I stay mad? He knew what I said I was going to do. The joke was on me. We sat and talked for three hours. I thanked her for giving me grounds for divorce; she apologized and then took pleasure in giving me details about their relationship, my personal business, and my family business. I continued to minister to her and lead her back to Christ. I got back in the house after 3:00 a.m., still laughing like my best friend was right beside me. He was.

ME. Really, Lord, no teeth?

> I do not call you servants any longer, for the servant does not know what his master is doing; but I have called you [My] friends, because I have revealed to you everything that I have heard from My Father. (John 15:15 AMP)

All-Knowing

I HAD AN ISSUE WHERE A hacker obtained access to my Wi-Fi network, and my personal information had been compromised. After receiving the runaround from CSRs, I requested my account be closed. I asked the representative when my contract was up.

REP. On your birthday.
ME. Hallelujah! Cancel it!

I was so happy. I knew I had the victory over the whole situation, and daily, God has worked everything together for my good. He even used that situation to bring birthday surprises my way. I have celebrated my birthday for the whole month, for as long as I can remember. This year was extra special, filled with surprises from God almost every day. He already knew what I needed to hear to cancel that contract.

> It shall also come to pass that before they call, I will answer; and while they are still speaking, I will hear. (Isaiah 65:24 AMP)

Adonai

ONE LOVELY AFTERNOON, WHILE SEATED in my parked car preparing to go to a church meeting, there was suddenly a thunderous presence. With immediate response, my spirit seemed to stand at attention while my flesh was still seated, as my skin quivered violently from my bones. I heard the voice of Sovereignty.

GOD. You will do what I tell you to do, go where I tell you to go, say
    what I tell you to say, and do not look at their faces.
ME. My Adonai!

I had no idea who Adonai was, yet my spirit acknowledged Him. As my body continued to shake uncontrollably, I reached into my glove compartment to get a book called *The Names of God*. The first name I came to was Adonai. Coincidence? Certainly not! Adonai is the plural of Adon, meaning "Lord" and "Master." Adonai calls us into ministry and equips us to perform the task.

Finally, I managed to get out of my car, while still shaking. I told the pastor what happened. It was confirmed in His Spirit, and we moved forward with the next steps toward preaching ministry. Hallelujah!

> If you will fear the LORD [with awe and profound reverence] and serve Him and listen to His voice and not rebel against His commandment, then both you and your king will follow the LORD your God [and it will be well]. (1 Samuel 12:24 AMP)

Cruise Director

I STARTED A TRAVEL BUSINESS FOR my birthday and prayed and asked God to help me become Disney certified so I could treat the family to a Disney cruise. I didn't get a response from the Lord, and eventually, I forgot about it. After all, I live a pretty busy life but always try to have an ear out for the voice of the Lord. Not many days later, a small patch of grass started to grow in front of my home that looked like Mickey Mouse. Lord! I laughed so hard.

ME. Thank You, Daddy. Thank You.

God is so good and funny too. He placed it in a spot where I couldn't miss it. The only grass that grew was in the shape of Mickey Mouse. He is too much!

> As for the rich in this present world, instruct them not to be conceited and arrogant, nor to set their hope on the uncertainty of riches, but on God, who richly and ceaselessly provides us with everything for our enjoyment. (1 Timothy 6:17 AMP)

I'm so glad Jesus is not religious; He thought to bless me with a cartoon on my lawn. I pray that our God would bless you with the special desires of your heart in a personal way today!

Tailor

I PURCHASED A ROBE AHEAD OF time for our consecration service, but my robe arrived very late. It was too late to return, and I was referred to a tailor for alterations.

My robe was ridiculously large. The arms were an additional full hand's length, and the bottom of the robe draped down to the floor. I was convinced that I had the wrong robe. A football player had my robe, and I had his.

I went to the home of the tailor, got my measurements taken, left the robe, and blessed the Lord for making a way. It took a week or more to get a response from the tailor. What was I to do? This robe experience was the worst!

I finally received a call and an apology for the delay. The tailor had death in his family an was out of town, so he could not work on my robe. I went to pick it up the day before my consecration service with tears in my eyes. He tacked it in a few places, and off I went to lay it on the church's altar and present it to the Lord.

The service was amazing, but I don't remember any words of encouragement from any of the leadership. The enemy was present and accounted for. All I heard were the hardships attached to being a prophet of God. I was confused and discouraged for days after the service.

GOD. Put on your robe, get on your face, and don't get up until you die yet another death.

There I lay, faced down, in a XXL robe. I was confused, disappointed, crying, and praying. Once I settled down and surrendered to my heart, the Lord spoke again.

GOD. What you've been seeing is theatrics. Now I'm going to show
you real ministry. I didn't allow you to alter your robe. If you
had altered your robe, you would have altered your ministry.

Well, Hallelujah!

> As for God, His way is blameless. The word
> of the Lord is tested [it is perfect, it is flawless];
> He is a shield to all who take refuge in Him.
> (Psalm 18:30 AMP)

About the Author

Charnette Kay is a consecrated prophet in the Lord's Church, operating with special grace in healing and deliverance ministry. Her passion is winning souls to the kingdom of God, preaching and teaching the Gospel of Jesus Christ, and encouraging the body of Christ to perfect their worship and cultivate their love relationship with God the Father, through His Son Jesus the Christ. Charnette is also a worshipper, who commands the atmosphere with the sound of heaven, a writer, a Christian life coach, and an overseer of King of Glory Ministries.